Hope For Freedom

The Essential Elements of Personal Ministry

By Jim & Pat Banks

By Jim Banks
www.houseofhealingministries.org
www.traumaprayer.com

Also authors of;

The Effects of Trauma and How to Deal with It, 3rd Edition
& A Workbook for the above title
The Insidious Dance, The Paralysis of Perfectionism
Finishing Well
One Calling, One Ministry
Defeating Jezebel
Finding Your Life's Calling
Helping Your Veteran Deal with The Effects of Trauma
Which Tree by Pat Banks
Loved to Transparency by Pat Banks
Boundaries
Choose Your Outcome w/ Mandy Valdes
Ministering to Victims of Sex Trafficking
Just Thinking
Cast A Long Shadow, Walking in The Kingdom
Angels and Demons

Chapter 1

An Introduction

Periodically Pat and I are asked a very simple question about our ministry; "What is it that you do?" Ordinarily, that would be an easy question to answer for most people, but we have used such a variety of tools over the years, and in many individual ministry sessions, that what we actually do, or rather how we do what we do, becomes difficult to describe. That is primarily because every personal ministry situation is different due to the wide variety of traumas, wounding, betrayals, abuse, family of origin, etc. and the unpredictable way individuals respond to them. It should be obvious that this would be the case because the people who come to us are so different, in spite of the many commonalities of their problems. However, over time we have become aware of a fundamental truth about woundedness and the traditional healing process that we felt we needed to distance ourselves and our clients from.

The harmful dynamic is this; If an individual focuses solely on healing wounds, then their expectation is that all of life is out in front of them somewhere waiting for them to get all their wounds healed before they can enter into the purpose for which they were created; if I can just get this wound healed, or rid of this pain, then everything will be better, etc. So too would personal fulfillment and some level of self-gratification as a result of engaging in their life calling be held at bay awaiting the final resolution. It's the way we humans see things; identify the end goal and then pursue it, even if it is so short sighted that it robs you of real life in the mean time.

But waiting for the day for 'real' life to begin to happen, or your ship to come in, or the day when all of your wounds are finally healed can be disheartening because the enemy is doing everything in his power to keep that from ever materializing, not to mention bringing new ones to deal with. We are well acquainted with the verse that says,

"Hope deferred makes the heart sick, but a desire fulfilled is a tree of life." Proverbs 13:12 (ESV)

What we have seen over decades of ministry activity should be of no surprise to anyone; the whole ulterior motive behind the enemy's attacks against each of us is to destroy, cripple, or so mar our personal identity through traumas, wounding, disappointment, rejection, disillusionment, betrayals, abuse, etc, to the point that we will not be led to engage in the purpose for which God created us, but will simply focus on getting our wounds healed. Our primarily motivation may be to simply diminish our personal pain, but the end goal for most folks is to remove the blockages that keep them from living life and achieving their dreams. If that's the goal it will be a frustrating journey.

Knowing that dynamic has caused us to refocus our attention so that our primary goal has become only dealing with those things that have damaged or clouded an appreciation of how each person was created such that they can readily embrace what they we were created for; purpose, in spite of all their wounds.

The restoration of personal identity and the realization of purpose creates a capacity to live life in spite of our personal handicaps, wounds, and contrary circumstances.

"Knowing the why for his existence ... (he) will be able to bear almost any how." Viktor Frankl, A Man's Search For Meaning, 1946 (Frankl spent 3 ½ years in a Nazi death camp during WWII.)

We now concentrate our efforts on helping people recover, or re-establish, their personal identity. When that is finally realized then individuals can move into experiencing real life without healing every last wound being the entire focus, but instead can begin to experience the fulfillment that comes from knowing why they were created and fully engaging in what they were created to do.

Yes, the wounds and emotional blockages, etc, still need to be addressed and healed but they will no longer be the blockages to their purpose that they once were because they will be able to pursue a much higher cause. As a result, their future will no longer be "out there somewhere" waiting for them to get healed, but they will be able to connect with it on a daily basis because the higher pursuit of purpose and expression of personal identity promotes vision and satisfaction.

Another significant element of that focus is that people can now begin to focus on relationships which as a result of wounding brought about voluntary isolation which either limited or totally cut off this much needed resource for recovery. It is much easier to begin to develop and mature in identity than to try and grow through woundedness.

To that end, we have also found that at the initiation of personal ministry many have found comfort in being provided some information about the structure of the process that they will be entering into, what their responsibilities will be, and what will be required of them to not only engage the healing process, but what is necessary to provide the maximum opportunity for the process to become the answer to the dilemma they have prayed for and diligently sought.

In the course of this process, there will be a number of specific assignments that each individual will be asked to do and there are a number of other things that as ministers we get to help them do.

Folks also need to know that we are not interested in a long-term ministry relationship with them. Yes, we would probably love to be long-term friends, but we don't want them to be dependent upon us for sustaining either their identity or their healing. Part of our goal is equip them with the insight and skills to do most of that on their own in the future as needed. There will always be a need for others to help any of us in our walk through this life, but as aides only, not as permanent fixtures in life.

If you choose to work with us, we pray that the healing and restoration process for you will also equip you with some of the tools to become a healer yourself. Often our best teacher is personal experience.

We trust that this brief introduction coupled with the following information herein outlined will give you some sense of the purpose, direction and structure of the ministry you are considering entering into, as well as help instill the confidence to stay in the process so that you may reap the rewards that hundreds have gained through our ministry over the last 30 years of personal ministry.

Blessings on your journey,

Jim and Pat Banks

www.houseofhealingministrie.org
www.traumaprayer.com

PS; Because we never know what presenting issues clients will bring to us to help them resolve, it is quite likely that we will not use a number of these tools in the healing and identity restoration process. However, we have chosen to cover them all so that you can see that there is a comprehensive set of tools available that we can call on if needed.

⏹

Chapter 2

The House of Healing Ministries

Personal Healing & Restoration Process Outline

Interview and the Ministry Questionnaire

Much of what follows in this healing and restoration process outline may not be presented in the actual order that you might personally experience it when you come to us for a personal ministry appointment because each individual and their difficulties are different indeed. In fact, in a personal ministry session with us, whether is is for a single 90 minute appointment or a one/two/three day Intensive ministry session, you may only experience two or three of the various elements noted herein. We are more dedicated to you making progress than we are to running through a check-list of things to do. However, everyone will start with this interview element.

Prior to actually beginning the personal ministry process, there will be a period of fact gathering so that we are both clear on what the issues are that are giving you trouble. The next piece we are looking to ascertain is how committed are you to solving this problem. You will need to be fully committed to solving the underlying issue(s) behind the difficulties you are experiencing, not simply wanting to feel better about what's going on.

Obviously, feeling better is certainly part of your motivation and we understand that and want to do what we can to make that happen. However, occasionally we run into someone who wants healing on their terms: they want to choose what to do and how to do it. That usually doesn't work well for us or our potential client because they normally not very self-aware as so want us to deal with things that will not be helpful to them in the long run.

When you go to a surgeon to remove a cancer from a vital organ, it's best not to try and supervise the operation.

Resolving the issues that are causing you to seek ministry will often require some hard work on your part. More often than not it means facing some fears that have kept real solutions at bay for a long time. If there are issues you still don't want to face, then our ability to help will be severely hampered, and frankly, we would rather not have to fight you to get you to do what you know you must do to become whole. Although the process may not be fun, the fear of dealing with it is often thought to be much greater than the actuality.

As we determine the range of issues that you are dealing with, the next thing we are looking to determine is if we are a good fit for you.

There are occasions when the issues people would like for us to solve are actually beyond our areas of expertise. We want to be honest with you, as well as with ourselves when we commit to work with you that we feel that we can make some real progress and not just spend time with you. If we are not a good fit for you then we would like to recognize it up front before you expend resources and we invest a lot of time just spinning our wheels. That's not fair to either of us and on occasion, the early interview process makes that clear for both of us.

Another factor that enters into our decision process is that we also do a fair amount of traveling to teach and train in other states and countries, which prevents us from working with people who need consistent weekly contact with us. We just do not want to make a commitment to you that we possibly cannot fulfill.

The first phase of this information acquisition process will be to have you go to our web site www.houseofhealingministries.org then download and print out the file noted as "Ministry Questionnaire." This is 23 pages of some very specific questions relating to your personal history, as well as what you know of the history of your family of origin. This information helps us deal with the roots of specific issues and high-lights patterns of family behaviors that need to be addressed.

Please pay attention to any dreams you have as you are filling out the form. This Questionnaire asks some very pointed questions that you might not want your immediate family members or roommates to be privy to. So as you are working on it protect it. Don't leave it round the house for anyone to pick up and read.

We would like to have the form filled out and sent to us well in advance of your appointment so that we can review and pray over it.

The second phase of information gathering will be a personal interview either face–to-face, or over Skype, Facetime, Zoom, or via the phone. The interaction will also simply allow us to have a better understanding of how the problem you are dealing with effects you and those around you. It may also serve to fill in any gaps in the information provided in the Questionnaire you have filled out and gives us additional understanding that we need to minister to you effectively.

?

Chapter 3

Stinking Thinking

(aka, You're Not Right In the Head)

Invariably when we are approached by individuals who are struggling and are asked to help them resolve the results of trauma and wounding from life's experiences, we immediately come face to face with some habit patterns that are obvious repercussions of the stuff they've been through and which they have yet to process properly. The chief of those is the demeaning way people think and talk about themselves; often the result of years of living with a victim spirit, an orphan or unloving spirit, or what we like to refer to as a spirit of self-hate.

The most effective way to change a bad habit is to do almost the exact opposite. But one cannot do that if he or she is not aware of the dysfunctional manner in which they actually treat themselves on a daily basis. We, humans, are intimately aware of where we made a mistake, did something wrong, could have tried harder, made a different decision, or shouldn't have done something or another. We know we should learn from our mistakes, so we berate ourselves for having messed up, then continually rehearse what we did wrong, over-and-over-and-over, ad nausium, as though that will sear it upon our conscience in such a manner that it will ensure that we'll never ever do that again.

The cold hard reality of it is we do learn from our mistakes because pain or embarrassment are very good teachers. There is no need to carry tons of self-imposed, guilt, shame and condemnation that needs frequent re-enforcement.

The world has taught us that if we are nice to people, they'll probably be nice to us. So we tend to treat everybody else on the planet better than we treat ourselves. That has to cease. We need to break those habits at least to the extent that we are treating ourselves as least as well as we treat everyone else.

The difficulty is that we are more comfortable living with regret, remorse and self-imposed guilt, shame and condemnation because we think we deserve it. It has also become a lifestyle for us.

This means that there is a necessity to break old habits and thought processes by regularly exercising some intentionality in speaking and thinking differently about ourselves. Consequently, there will be some exercises that you will have to engage to build new, more healthy ways of speaking to and thinking about yourself. Make no mistake about it, old habits die hard, but this one has to go.

It is a choice that must be made in order get out of the hole you and the enemy have dug.

"We who lived in concentration camps can remember men who walked through the huts comforting others, giving away their last piece of bread. They may have been few in number, but they off sufficient proof that everything can be taken from a man but one thing: the last of the human freedoms – to choose one's attitude in any given set of circumstances, to choose one's own way." Experiences in a Concentration Camp, Viktor Frankl

You have a choice. You can continue to live in a concentration camp of your own making, or you can make another choice and live free of your own condemnation. Correcting your self-talk may be one of the assignments we ask you to engage.

There are also many other ramifications of performance and perfectionism that can result in similar issues that personal ministry will address. It your situation warrants we may suggest some specific reading assignments for you to complete prior to or during the course of personal ministry. It will all be designed to help you change the way you think and speak about yourself.

Proverbs 23:7 "For as a man thinketh in his heart, so is he:" (KJV)

One of the other assignments we may give you has to do with expressions of the heart for those you love and are significantly connected or bonded to.

One of the most common effects of abuse and traumatic events, or a lifestyle of abuse, is the activity in the pre-frontal cortex of our brain begins to decrease and move to the back of the brain. The pre-frontal cortex is where complex issues are examined and our relational circuits are located, which enable us to resolve sticky complicated issues, which are most often problems with a significant relational component to them. The back of the brain handles all issues related to basic survival needs; a warm dry place to sleep, food & water intake, clothing and sex, etc. which are exacerbated by isolation, which is also common for trauma sufferers.

The process of recovering lost brain activity requires that one must intentionally embrace the activity of frequent verbal expressions of gratitude and appreciation – face to face with other humans, not your dog. Your pet may be deeply appreciative of your attention, but it will not be a help to you. Expressing appreciation for someone to them directly has the added effect of facing the fear of rejection, renewing bonded relationships and expressions of trust and connection which are essential for building the relational connectivity needed for healing and sustaining it after the initial healing process has been completed.

You may start off by making those expressions to third parties who don't personally know those you are expressing appreciation for. If you stay with this exercise, in time you will be able to express it directly to those that you need to hear it. But regardless of whether they are able to hear it or not, restoration of activity in the pre-frontal cortex will begin to surface in a positive manner; you'll be able to make better decisions, discernment will become more refined and formerly impossible problems will begin to find solutions.

Another essential skill that is needed, which will be an assignment if needed, is personal emotional awareness.

One of the common results of abuse, trauma and deep wounding, especially when it begins at a young age, is that many find their emotions too difficult to handle and find themselves easily overwhelmed by them. This dynamic causes people to stuff, hide or deny them so to avoid being overwhelmed. It didn't help that at the time their parents seldom, if ever, realized what's going on in their children's lives and that tended to make them feel they were unprepared to deal with their own emotions. It was often easier to tell children to get over it and move on. Since the magnitude of youthful emotions can often become debilitating when misunderstood causes children, even young adults, to feel, out of control, embarrassed, or betrayed by them. It's easier just to stuff them.

As we have seen a great deal of recently, reaching adulthood then becomes problematic when feelings of frustration, anger, or depression are experienced without the ability to distinguish what they are, when he/she have never taken the opportunity to stop and find out why they are feel that way. Unresolved emotional confusion is a recipe for misery because we were created with emotions being an integral part of our functioning. Choosing to live without emotions also results in a choice to give up our voice (authority and our place) in relationships and community.

Continuing to live in denial of our God-given emotions is also a major block to progress in healing and must be addressed. It's rather like an itch you can't scratch. You know you need change, but you can't access it, and because you can't feel much of anything but anger and fear, you wouldn't know you had it if you actually got it.

Consequently, we have to forcibly stop ourselves when these feeling arise and listen to our own voice. This means we are going to have to intentionally face our fears and enter a process of becoming aware of our emotions and try to precisely define them by putting an accurate name on them … and try to determine what triggered them.

For many, this is a major step in acquiring freedom because we become acquainted with an internal resource we have never drawn on before that is quite capable in managing the fear of becoming exposed, embarrassed and out of control: the recovery of our voice and our authority.

Your emotions and how you engage them and engage others with them is also a significant key in the determination of personal identity. Consequently, we are keen to see you engage life with your emotions intact as an integral part of the package.

🛇

Chapter 4

Personal Wiring Appreciation

Pat and I are big believers in understanding how the Lord wired us from the day He created us. That wiring determines how we see information and situations, how we handle relationships, how we interact socially, as well as forms and sustains our world view. You can observe the difference in individual wiring by how toddlers act in a pre-school or nursery environment. One will want to tell everybody how to play, another will want to do nothing but build things, another will instantly drop what they are doing to go comfort a playmate that has fallen and is crying, while another is content to sit in a corners and look at books.

There are many personality tests running around these days; Life Languages, Enneagram, Strength Finders, Meyers-Briggs, etc. Each can provide additional insight into why we do things as we do, but personalities change and strengths wax and wane as we progress to and through various stages of life, which is why Pat and I prefer to educate those we work with in Redemptive Gifts, an observation of human behavior created by Arthur Burk (www.theslg.com) and is well founded in scripture.

The reason we prefer to use this specific tool is two-fold. First of all, our wiring does not change with age, circumstance or gifting. It can certainly be enhanced by successful parenting or suppressed by our parents if they have been wounded by authorities in their lives who were very immature in the same wiring, but it fundamentally will always be discernible throughout their lives.

Secondly, we prefer to use it because it is one of the few tools that goes far beyond explaining why we think and act as we do, to pointing out what specific areas we need to grow or mature in.

Quite often we find the source of most marital problems stem from the fact that neither of the parties are aware of their own wiring, much less the potential conflicts that arise because their spouse's wiring. The fact of the matter is we never marry nor are we attracted to someone exactly like us. It is the differences that can be both initially alluring and intriguing, and eventually annoying.

Scripture admonishes men to, live with their wives in an "understanding way." Meaning that a man should study his wife's behavior and wiring so that he may minimize the effects of the personal conflicts that arise, perhaps even avoid them: for understanding creates grace to accept certain characteristics because they are actually from God Himself.

We have found with hundreds of people that we've ministered to that understanding how you are wired gives people a great deal of insight not into why they think, process and act as they do, and why they are interested and drawn to certain activities as they are. These are all connected to individual purpose.

The ability to consistently be engaged in our purpose is by divine design, but it won't be consistently fulfilling if we choose not to mature in our wiring; neither will our relationships. Understanding Redemptive Gifts has saved numerous marriages, as well as business careers.

Proverbs 4:7 "Wisdom is the principal thing; therefore get wisdom: and with all thy getting get understanding." (KJV)

Because understanding your individual wiring is a huge key to establishing or the recovery of your personal identity, we are quite anxious for you to discover your unique wiring. During the process, you will also learn a great deal about how others are wired and the potential conflicts that arise as a result of our differences. This understanding will help mitigate a number of relational roadblocks that occur because of a lack of grace for the differences that exist. The new information has also saved a number of marriages over the years as we have introduced couples to it.

Chapter 5

Eliminating the Consequences of Sin and Bad Decisions

This is what we call legal work. It is the simple process of canceling all of the legal reasons we and others have given to the enemy to torture and torment us mentally and spiritually.

Proverbs 26:2 "As the bird by wandering, as the swallow by flying, so the curse causeless shall not come." (KJV)

Demons are opportunists. Where ever and whenever there is sin a demon will show up try to create a stronghold in anyone's life. We use a number of tools to break their hold and remove the reason that the demon came in the first place. One of the easiest way to accomplish this is found in the information presented in the last half dozen pages of the Ministry Questionnaire that asks you, via a check-the-box format, to detail the specific sins you committed. In general they are: lack of forgiveness, word curse spoken by others and yourself, vows that you have made, resentment and unforgiveness that you still hang on to, judgments you have made, issues with authorities, self-imposed guilt, shame and condemnation that you are still carrying, soul ties that have gone unbroken, and demonic attachments that you can identify in your family line through recurring difficulties, etc.

Another important thing that we all need to break are what the Bible calls Iniquities. Now iniquities are not sin, they are however as bad as sin because these are the family prides, prejudices and dysfunctional beliefs that cause us to sin. They are often the thing we have either been taught by members of our family of origin, by the baser elements of our culture and opinions formed by negative circumstances, or the funky belief systems we have a embraced. Some pertinent examples are: how we think of and treat members of the opposite sex, attitudes toward alcohol, how we do or do not practice honor, viewpoints of those from other races or countries or even people of different educational levels or social status, how we think of and handle money, and unfortunately in our divisive political climate how we view those who align with another political party.

These iniquitous beliefs systems are often the forces behind prejudices, discrimination, and separatism. They can also promote poverty and distrust of institutional structures that can benefit us greatly if properly engaged. It even influences the way we see the value of people of different cultures and religions.

As someone has said, "You never know what's in the bottom of the cup until it's shaken." These attitudes may be indiscernible until pressure is applied. Then the volcano that has existed undetected under the surface for decades erupts and spews it defilement over everyone in the vicinity. Our news feeds are full of such actions.

These are the things we want to uncover and disarm and doing all the legal work necessary to remove the permission we knowingly or unknowingly gave the enemy and his demonic minions is part of the process of becoming free.

It also frequently has the added benefit of revealing those root belief systems that have hampered our ability to do the very thing we want to do and yet have found ourselves either self-sabotaging, or simply unable to muster the commitment to do them, which has become the major blockage to progress in all manner of areas in life.

This one of the reasons why the Ministry Questionnaire asks so many pointed questions. If you have demons oppressing, depressing, impressing or otherwise influencing your thoughts or actions, we want to help you remove it so that you can flourish.

⁇

Chapter 6

The Healing Stuff

I have used this analogy for years, and I think it still bears repeating because for many people it explains something they have never understood about the process of healing that they not only needed to know but have mistakenly been disappointed (even angry) because the healing did n't overtake them. After all, they had done everything they were supposed to do and it didn't happen.

If a father were to give his 3 year old son a pair of snazzy cowboy boots for his birthday, the delighted youngster will naturally, and happily, walk around kicking things. They are perfect for that because their toes don't get hurt when they do it.

The next morning following his birthday celebration junior dons his boots and walks into the kitchen and says, "Hi, mom!" at the same time giving her a swift kick in the ankle, fully expecting her to be as impressed with his new boots as he is. But mom's reaction is totally different than he ever anticipated. Mom shrieks in pain and begins hopping around the kitchen on one leg trying not to simultaneously wet her pants, or hit her son with a frying pan.

Junior realizes what he's done and genuinely says, "I'm sorry mommy, I'm sorry!" perfectly fulfilling the Biblical requirement to seek forgiveness for injuries inflicted upon another, deeply offending them in the process. (Matthew 5:23)

Mom says, "I forgive you!" and actually means it, fulfilling another Biblical command; if you refuse to forgive others then the Lord will refuse to forgive you. (Matthew 6:14-15) Now ... this I ask you ... everyone has done what they were supposed to do, ask forgiveness and extend forgiveness, does her pain immediately stop?

The obvious answer is, NO!

However, what we have been taught by implication is that forgiving equals healing. Unfortunately, that is wrong. Forgiveness is sometimes accompanied by healing for the wound inflicted, but only sometimes. Generally speaking, there are two processes involved. First is pronouncement of forgiveness, which unbinds the offended from the offender, or the abused from the abuser, as well as from the event itself. The second is the process of healing which must be intentionally entered.

When Jesus announced the initiation of His ministry in Isaiah 61:1, he said,

"The Spirit of the Lord GOD is upon me, because the LORD has anointed me to bring good news to the poor (forgiveness); he has sent me to bind up the brokenhearted (healing), to proclaim liberty to the captives (freedom), and the opening of the prison to those who are bound (freedom from bondage);"

Notice the progression, forgiveness (good news), then healing (tending/mending a broken heart) then freedom from bondage. The cool thing is that this is a quotation of an Old Testament passage the fullness of which was not possible without the opening phrase (fifteen word) of Isaiah 61:1 being made possible by the death, burial and resurrection of Jesus Christ, whose spirit would now be made available to all enabling this verse to become an actuality for each of us.

Notice also the two terms He specifically used: captive and prisoner. Captives are in a prison through no fault of their own (think sexual abuse victim), while a prisoner is in prison for something that he did do (think abuser). The same freedom is made available to both through Jesus Christ if they will seek it.

The healing, or binding up of the broken heart, is acquired through your direct engagement with Jesus Christ (with our assistance) so that true healing and restoration occurs. We have embraced a number of tools that will specifically allow you, the victim or the victimizer, to find freedom, to experience healing and release from the bondages that have made life so miserable through engaging the presence of God.

If this is unfamiliar to you, don't get all uptight about it. You will actually find it very natural and very rewarding to find that Jesus actually meant it when Jesus said,

> "My sheep hear my voice, and I know them, and they follow me." John 10:27

> "... the words that I speak unto you, they are spirit, and they are life." John 6:63b

Religion has not been kind to us in that it has implied that the only ones who hear from God are those special characters that we call pastors and priests – folks who are called from the cradle to full time service unto the Lord, set apart like Jeremiah.

And we've been fine with that, for, after all, we have to make a living, engage in a life-long career challenges, mind our health, service debt, raise kids and do all that adulting stuff.

Religion raised the bar further when it declared that God has spoken once, and once only through the Bible.

But when Jesus was introduced to us by the angels they said He would be called "Emmanuel" which means "God with us," not God among us, God observing us, or God contained in a book He'll send you. In John 17:20-21 we find an even more intimate statement,

> 20 "I (Jesus) do not ask for these (His disciples) only, but also for those (you and me) who will believe in me through their word,
>
> 21 that they (you and I) may all be one, just as you, Father, are in me, and I in you, that they (all of us) also may be in us, so that the world may believe that you have sent me".

Even though He is in me and I in Him, the fact of the matter is that I could say everything that Jesus would like to say to you, but it would likely have no great effect, it would not carry the weight or power to change things for you. In John 6:63 Jesus makes clear the difference between humans speaking and when He speaks,

> "It is the spirit that quicken (makes alive); the flesh profits nothing: the words that I (Jesus) speak unto you, they are spirit, and they are life." (KJV)

Consequently, this particular element of the healing process actually has two functions in it. First, it allows you to engage the

Lord directly for healing, but secondly, the process is also intent on familiarizing you with His voice, such that you are able to hear it and distinguish it from all the other voices that are competing for your time and attention – for the rest of your life.

For those of you who have either struggled to hear His voice or been fooled by the enemy into thinking you heard His voice and heard all manner of condemning junk, we'll help fix that for you because too, for He's looking for you to enter a new depth of relationship with Him where the promise of John 15:15-16 is yours in entirety;

> 15 *"No longer do I call you servants, for the servant, does not know what his master is doing; but I have called you friends, for all that I have heard from my Father I have made known to you.*
>
> 16 *You did not choose me, but I chose you and appointed you that you should go and bear fruit and that your fruit should abide, so that whatever you ask the Father in my name, he may give it to you."*

Being a friend of God is not only the desire that we hold before ourselves continually, but we pray that all those we minister to will likewise adopt this same heart and that they will be able to quickly enter into a sustainable level of relational intimacy with the Lord that will carry them throughout the balance of their lives, as well as through life's future trials and tribulations.

We would also encourage you to strictly avoid any ministry who's declared goal does not include these last two items. God is totally relational and He's not into perfection. There's only been one of those and He doesn't need another. He's simply interested in love and relationship.

Chapter 7

Removing Curses and Demonic Assignments

It should be obvious, even to the most casual of observers that since we live in a fallen world we are subject to demonic influence, both from within and without. No healing process would be effective (or complete) without removing the sources of those influences.

Some of these demonic influences and attachments were formed by living in a prolonged state of victimhood such that demonic attachment to pain and personal identity are formed.

Some of this may be the direct result of abuse, assignments by those who have been demonized themselves and were purposefully assigned to you.

Some of it may be the result of attachments secured by your own personal dysfunctional coping mechanisms, or your own misguided attempts to protect yourself from further abuse and victimizations that have backfired and made life more difficult.

Then there are always the consequences of our own ungodly choices. Willful sin and stupid decisions invariably require us to pay a great price. Occasionally, that price tag includes demonic attachments that form behavioral strongholds that can plague us till the day we die, and even get passed on to multiple succeeding generations without our permission.

Then too there is always the presence of some level of oppression that we live under 24/7 as a result of the environment we live in, which is ruled by satan's minions, along with sin's defilement of people and land. There are also the presence and activity of ruling demonic spirits covering a local area, a region or an entire nation.

I remember years ago I was trying to make a living in Orange County, CA selling sailboats. It was new and exciting for a while, but before long I could feel that something wasn't right but I just couldn't put my finger on it. I got assigned one day to ferry a 30 footer up from San Diego to our brokerage dock in Newport Beach. On the drive down there we (Pat and I) both had this sudden release from an amazingly heavy level of oppression right after crossing the Orange County line into San Diego County. It was so noticeable that both of us were immediately aware of it. We could breathe easier, as though a huge weight had suddenly been lifted from our chests.

It is sad, but often the oppression of the enemy is so subtle and increases so imperceptibly that we are not aware of how significant it is until we walk into a new geographic area.

Most of the activity involved in removing curses and demonic assignments comes from information about our ancestors and from a list of the symptoms of your situation: the blockages, torment, struggles, health issues and difficulties you are facing. They are easy to take care of. However, you can't just fire a shotgun blast into the netherworld hoping to hit something and expect to accomplish anything. One has to be fairly specific about what you are dealing with, and why you are dealing with it.

Some of them are fairly obvious, such as curses coming from having your ancestors (even multiple generations of ancestors) involved in Freemasonry and/or Eastern Star; past involvements in satanic cults and secret societies by you and/or your ancestors; victimization through satanic ritual abuse; all manner of other forbidden activities, such as conjuring up and consulting the spirits of the dead, etc. Viet Nam war veterans and Iraq War veterans were all cursed by Buddhist priests and Islamic Imams invoking the power of ancient demonic spirits to do the work.

There may also be a number of other demonic influences and oppressions that are impacting you that have been inspired by others that need to be taken care of, such as friends or acquaintances that are practicing witchcraft for purposes of manipulation or control; individuals who are jealous of you and if you are in ministry or connected to a church (pastoral staff) then you will have to deal with local coven activity against the Body of Christ of which you are a part.

Most, if not all of the information needed to cut these nasty buggers off will be contained in the information you provide in the Ministry Questionnaire, or through our personal interview. The Holy Spirit is also interested in seeing that you walk free and has a much better information base and a much better memory than either of us.

[?]

Chapter 8

Ministry to The Human Spirit

This is another tool that we are so glad that we embraced. This tool all by itself has been responsible for more progress for traumatized and deeply wounded people than anything else we have employed. It has the ability to touch people profoundly at a foundational level and is able to build capacity quicker than anything we else we have used. So you can expect that you may encounter it at some point in the healing and restoration process.

The power of it lays in the fact that we were created in the image of God. Since God is a Spirit (John 14), you and I were created as spirits as well, and we should operate primarily through our human spirit (being subject of course, to the Spirit of God.) When God created us He vested a small portion of Himself in us, and it is that unique combination of things he also put in us (as a result of our specific purpose for being created) which includes our personal identity.

The enemy has done some really nasty things to people because he hates God and His prized creation (you and me.) He also knows that you and I have been sent here to accomplish some specific things that only you and I can accomplish. The easiest way for the enemy to upset God's apple cart is to somehow damage you and your identity so that rather than be about the business you were created for, you'll spend all your time either trying to get healed, or you will engage something else with your life because you didn't know who you are. As the old adage goes, "If you don't know where you're going, any road will take you there." For many of us, that road had a lot of forks in it that lent itself well to an excessive number of detours. In many cases, the resulting choices we made only contributed to our dysfunction and misery.

I (Jim) know this first hand because there were many decisions I made whose motivation was questionable. For instance, I went to college and studied electrical engineering. After college, I started working for a consulting engineering company in Houston, TX only to find out that I hated design engineering. Making decisions for purely practical reasons seldom works out well and that little detour introduced a 3 and ½ year delay in getting on with life. If personal identity is not settled finding purpose is equally elusive.

Certain traumas, particularly rejections and abandonment early in life, tend to do something similar except they leave wounds not only in the soul but in the human spirit as well. What that does to development is to reduce the capacity to recover quickly making future traumas and prolonged difficulties even more problematic.

Over the years we have noticed that people who have wounded spirits are not well able to sustain their healing for an extended period of time regardless of what healing they have acquired in their souls. That makes ministry to the human spirit even more important.

Because the human spirit is the residence of both identity and purpose, as well as connectivity with the Spirit of God, it is important to address it relatively early in the healing process. The great part about this tool is that the recipient of the ministry doesn't have to do anything but hold the gaze of the minister. He or she does all the work.

I (Jim) had a woman come to work with me several years ago whose spirit was heavily damaged. This woman had experienced about every trauma a female could experience. She had been raped three times, two of them at gunpoint, robbed at gunpoint on two other occasions, beaten unconscious three times by her first husband, pushed out of a moving car by her second husband, unable to work and lived on a meager disability check in subsidized housing in a bad part of town.

She was somewhere in her late 40's, morbidly obese, walked with the aid of two metal forearm crutches and was so afraid of men that she would not come without a couple being with her. When they arrived I was told by her chaperones that she would only be able to visit with me for about 15 minutes, for that's all the energy she had. What can anyone do for another in only 15 minutes?

So I asked that question of Holy Spirit and the answer I got was minister to her human spirit. So I did and whatever demon she had would cause her to simply pass out at the 15-minute mark. She would conk out and then after a few minutes, I would check to see if she was still breathing then step out. We went through this strange exercise once a week for about a month. With each succeeding visit, she gained a bit of capacity and a bit more light in her eyes.

By week number seven she was able to trust me enough to come alone and we dealt with the first rape, which she said was the first time she had ever told anyone about it. Somewhere in there, I dealt with the weirdo demon that caused her to pass out every time she came, so I never had to check to see if she was breathing again.

We had a couple more visits then she got ill and we started a series of training trips out of state and I lost contact with her.

About a year later, my wife and I were back in town again and stopped at a grocery store we don't usually visit to pick up a couple of items. As we parked and were getting out of the car this same woman came trotting up to us to say hello. I didn't recognize her initially because she'd lost about 100 pounds, but was still using the forearm crutches and dressed about the same. She was smiling, seemed to be full of life and actually appeared to be happy, none of which had I ever witnessed before. She thanked me profusely and gave us a quick update on her life and activities. She wasn't anywhere near the same woman I remembered working with.

Such is the power of ministry to the spirit.

The other thing that is so powerful about ministry to the human spirit is that within it is personal identity. It knows why you are here and what you have been sent to do. In most cases, it has had to retreat behind the soul (mind, will and emotions) and kind of hang out, and watch soul do its thing. Ministry to it is life and food which nurtures it and will bring it to the forefront of your being. This is when life can really begin because it is who you are, and being vitally connected to Holy Spirit there is nothing you are incapable of doing.

Chapter 9

Uncovering The Lies

As an adjunct to Chapter 3, there is always an emphasis on finding the lies you believe that the enemy has sown during your trials and tribulations during your time here on planet earth.

Do not be conformed to this world, but be transformed by the renewal of your mind, that by testing you may discern what is the will of God, what is good and acceptable and perfect." Romans 12:2 (ESV)

If the enemy has ever been good at anything this is it.

In the middle of every trauma, every failure, every mistake, and every emotionally charged event, the enemy comes to feed you a lie. It is always the same: a lie about you, a lie about God and a lie about those involved in what happened.

The fundamental lie about you that is commonly encountered is obviously negative, and it is always pointed directly at your personal value: I am not enough, and a million other perturbations of it such as; I am not good enough, smart enough, quick enough, I can't do WXYZ, I'll never be loved, provided for, or I deserve to poor, etc. Notice the first person expression of all these lies. This is how the enemy always expresses them to you in the midst of an emotional incident. It's not your original thought, but if you take it and repeat it, it's your new truth and it creates your reality. It's not THE truth, but it is now your truth. You are simply repeating what you've been told is your truth.

The process for renewing your mind begins with the discovery of the lies that you believe about yourself. A great many people are well aware of a couple of them because they've been in the back of their mind for decades – that small voice that says, "I can't lean this" or "I won't remember that" or my personal favorite, "I'd better not try that because I'll fail doing it and I can't have that!"

At other times we have to rely on God to show them to you because they are so intertwined with the way you see and process things that you are totally unaware of the wrong way you view issues. This why King David prayed this simple, yet profound prayer asking the Lord to uncover the hidden motivations and funky belief systems he had founded his life upon,

"Search me, O God, and know my heart! Try me and know my thoughts!

24 And see if there be any grievous way in me, and lead me in the way everlasting! Psalms 139:23-24 (ESV)

You see, in many cases, we cannot address the things we can neither see or don't understand because the misconceptions we are working under that shape how we conduct our lives and relationships are all we've ever known and I naturally assume that that's the way everybody else sees them as well. In order to live our lives as we were created we have to live in complete truth, not a half-truth, and the world we live in has worked very hard to corrupt the truth and keep you from living from it.

As a consequence, we spend quite a bit of our time and efforts in this area helping you get with the One who knows exactly how to unravel the web of lies you believe about yourself and how it cripples or hampers your efforts to be the best you can be.

⁇

Chapter 10

Performance Orientation

Since we live in such a performance-oriented society where value and acceptance are predicated on how well you perform there may well be reason to have to deal with perfectionism in order to resolve the issues surrounding your identity.

The biggest problem with perfectionism is that it is, in essence, an agreement with the teachings, principles, rules, and regulations of the system of the world. It is founded in fear and therefore has all manner of traps and unrealized consequences that are shrouded in virtually unrealizable promises. And yet one of our greatest internal drives is to be appreciated and valued, which is essentially what keeps us in this fruitless game.

Make no mistake about it, the system of the world will for a time reward you for following its principles, rules, and regulations, but it is a cruel taskmaster and its ultimate goal is to totally conform you to it, rather than the loving embrace of the Kingdom of God.

Perhaps two of the most devastating consequences of perfectionism are forcing you to abandon living from your heart in favor of living life out of the strength of your own mind, and the other, placing your value and acceptance in the hands of others.

Creativity is ultimately a spirit or heart driven exercise, whether it's in business, art, engineering, sports, dance, farming or personnel management. It is where true out of the box expressions of inspired problem solving come from, including navigating the conduct of difficult relationships that require insights that are beyond your knowledge and experience. Living life out of your head, as magnificent as it is, keeps you functioning out of what you know and what you have seen, essentially out of the limitations of your experience.

And since performing well is the means whereby perfectionism creates and establishes personal value, which requires you navigate all the pitfalls through the current extent of knowledge and experience in these matters that you have, failure is often a constant companion. So our personal view of our value is generally negative, although our minds will never let us acknowledge it publicly, which is in direct opposition to what we unconsciously feel.

God loves how He made you and He loves the purpose for which He made you. Consequently, our struggle is to remove the lies, half-truths and dysfunctional processes that keep our estimation of who we are, along with our personal worth and social value in opposition to His. That's what we get to help you resolve.

②

Chapter 11

Community (social trust avoidance & isolation)

I am a firm believer that becoming whole is made much more difficult outside of community. The enemy certainly knew that since he also knew that we were created for love and relationship, both with each other and with the Lord. So to counter relationship he brought fear to the table. When we are wounded the first thing we do is withdraw from community for a number of reasons.

First of all, the system of this world has caused us to buy into several beliefs all of which are fundamental extensions of performance orientation.

The first is, "**If I do right, everything will be right**." Certainly, there is some measure of truth in this statement but it not the whole truth. If you buy into this as your fundamental truth then what is the corollary? If I do wrong, everything will go wrong? In reality, it is more like, "If things go wrong for me, then I am wrong. (Code for there's probably something with me.) is that right? Hardly! But the system of the world insists that we each derive our value from doing things right, therefore being right. So if something goes wrong, the implication is that there is something wrong with me, which probably can't be fixed.

If that is my belief system then when something goes wrong in my life I will withdraw, because of the shame that goes along with failure.

The Catch 22 in the whole performance orientation is ratified in the presence of Murphy's Law, which states, "If there is the most remote possibility that something can go wrong, that ensures that it will go wrong." And furthermore, "The magnitude of the probability that something will go wrong is in direct proportion to the importance of the task or project, or my need for things to go right."

Another couple of reasons we retreat from community when we are experiencing tough times is; a) we live among a bunch of do-gooders who feel the need to give all manner of not-so-helpful advice – and we hate that, and b) we quickly grow weary of telling people the reason behind why we are not our usual peppy selves, and c) seeing others who are doing well only accentuates the depth of our troubles.

From another angle, we see that this is the handiwork of the enemy who has for millennia been working to sabotage everything that God and man try to accomplish. When the enemy cannot do it directly then he must pervert the minds of men and women to do it for him. We wonder why cancer takes so many lives and yet the answer is right before our eyes: our food, air, soil, and water are not what they were only 50 years ago. People have been eating bread for 5,000 years and suddenly 20% of our population is now allergic to it.

Another thing that humans respond to is the belief that, "Might makes right." In other words, "If I am right then I have power over those who are not." What does that say to the poor fellow who doesn't win all the time? Essentially, that those who win are superior and they have power over them. Is that true? Not in the least, unless that's what you believe, then it's your truth.

It is also at the core of the great political divide we are currently experiencing wherein people have taken the stance that what they believe and what they desire is morally superior to the positions of others. Consequently, all civil discourse has become its victim.

None of these ideas or belief systems promote community and to whatever degree that you ascribe to them you will experience separation, personal isolation, and loneliness. The diversity that makes community valuable is that which is necessary for wholeness because it is only in the context of a variegated community (relationship) that our crude ideals, funky belief systems, and poor attitudes can be confronted in love and our resulting relational dysfunction can be addressed.

What you also have to understand is that 'community' is not a weekly meeting. It is living out your normal everyday life among other people, preferably in a multi-generational setting. This means going shopping, church, lunch, work, going to high school football games and soccer matches, a neighbor's piano recital, community plays and concerts, County fairs and city celebrations and festivals. It means living all of your life in the company of others.

It may be scheduled around a weekly meeting for the sake of continuity, but most of life (except for work) is not scheduled. It happens somewhat spontaneously. That requires you to be flexible – in some sense, laying down how you would prefer to do things in order to experience life with other people.

Community has rights, which we enjoy, but it also has responsibilities. That means you are going to have to choose to not only participate in it regularly, but you are going to have to initiate dinners or informal social gatherings – you are going to have become (even if you have to force yourself) hospitable. You don't have to fund it, you simply need to be the organizer.

Community only thrives in the company of one another. And there is perhaps no greater community builder and nurturer than sharing a meal. Mealtime is holy to the Lord as demonstrated by the number of meals the Jesus was recorded to have had with His disciples. It is also the activities during which bonding occurs; initially with our mother and then with our family. If you want to practice hospitality in a holy atmosphere, sharing a meal with people you want to connect with is the best way.

Perhaps the greatest way to integrate yourself into a local community is through joining a local group that is involved in supporting a cause, or that is addressing a problem that they care deeply about. A unified purpose that requires some effort and faces some obstacles is one of the most effective means of bonding people together. For in these groups personal desires have to take a back seat to the greater call of purpose.

If that's not your cup of tea, then you may want to consider engaging in a hobby that requires you to also engage with other people. Common interest (or affinity groups) can also be an opportunity for community to build and for you to find a place in it. There is a level of sharing knowledge and experience in the context of whatever the hobby is that provides ample opportunity to bond with people you wouldn't ordinarily rub shoulders with.

Sailing was one of those things that I enjoyed. I was always embraced when I showed up at a new club for a race, or when you ran into another small group of sailors you didn't know. They instantly wanted to know who you were, where you were from, what equipment you boat had on it and how you rigged it. That was just the jumping off place for conversation and friendship formation.

One of the foundations of community is that to really benefit from it and enjoy all that it has to offer is that we have to learn some very important lessons that are essential for a happy productive life; to trust that others are growing in their struggle through life just as you are, to be forgiving not for a season but as a lifestyle, and to be an permanent intentional participant in it. To incorporate all of that into the healing process makes the journey complete and part of the joy of it is that those who witness it will celebrate it along with you.

Now I also want to address another aspect of community that seems to be a hot topic right now, that of finding your tribe. What is your tribe? Essentially it is a community that shares like values embrace healing and is dedicated to serving God in all that it says and does. It should call us to a higher standard of living, one of faith and generosity, of prayer and service, of humility and hospitality. You and I are to be woven into the fabric of that community so that our strengths bring support to it and so that our weaknesses or immaturity may be strengthened and matured.

Where is it? In many cases, it is you that determined where it is. As believers, we are generally far too dependent upon everyone else to provide what we think we need and are discouraged when we can't seem to find it. There are times and season when what we need is there for us. There are, however, more times and seasons of life wherein we must be the catalyst for the formation of that community otherwise we will be without it.

It is essential that we either find that community or be the one who raises the flag and says, "Rally around me, we're gonna do this thing!" Why? Because you and I cannot achieve what we were created to do outside of that community, or our tribe of people. Perhaps John Donne said it most succinctly when he wrote, "No man is an island. No one is self-sufficient; everyone relies on others." (Devotions, 1624)

?

Who Are We?

Jim Banks was trained as an electrical engineer and worked for several years as a design engineer for power systems for both office buildings and manufacturing plants through consulting engineering firms. He also worked in technical sales and marketing management for several industrial measurement and control equipment manufacturers.

Pat Banks worked for Bell telephone company as an executive trainer and later as an office manager for a Christian ministry in Colorado. They entered ministry full time in 2002 and are ordained through two ministry organizations.

The origins of their personal ministry began about 35 years ago while working full time, they became very frustrated while trying to help a number of young adult couples that they were in relationship with. It seemed that their limitations of skills and tools, along with their lack of training in their gifting allowed them only the ability to pick them up, dust them off, put on a band-aid or two, then send them out for another dose of the same, only to have to do it all over again within a couple of months.

This propelled them on to what has become a lifelong journey of learning and adding other healing tools to their belt. As they became better educated and more experienced, they began doing Inner Healing & Deliverance out of their home in an attempt to help those around them reach their full potential with God. What began as a couple of nights a week, quickly grew into both nights and weekends while working full time, eventually becoming a full-time endeavor in 2002.

In the succeeding years, they have helped thousands of people finally bring an end to their personal and family suffering and find healing for the wounded and broken places in their lives. Many have found release from the trauma of rape, physical, emotional and sexual abuse, and on occasion have been healed of some physical issue related to the trauma as well.

Marriages have been restored and family estrangements ended. Many have found that as childhood wounds were healed, the fears and anxieties released, emotional freedom was realized, along with relief from physical problems and other afflictions such as depression, stomach disorders, fibromyalgia, chronic fatigue, tormenting dreams, sleep deprivation and many other chronic ailments routinely disappear.

The original 23-minute audio recording of the Trauma Prayer available on Youtube.com and other websites has reached over a million people and has been heard in virtually every country on earth. About 20,000 people fall asleep to it every night. Since that original recording, several other versions have been added specifically to prominent types of trauma, such as PTSD for returning combat veterans.

The prayers have even helpful for hundreds of people who have listened to it but couldn't understand it because they didn't speak English.

Individual prayer ministry from them is available on an appointment basis in a comfortable, secure private setting in their local office. They will also minister via Skype and other digital means.

The Banks also do a great deal of training in the US and engage in personal ministry for missionaries around the world and have worked closely with several missions organizations. To arrange for a personal ministry session, or a one, two or three day intensive, you can contact them through their website at www.houseofhealingministries.org or www.traumaprayer.com.

Pat and Jim have four married children living all over the Eastern half of the US and currently have six grandchildren.

The easiest way to Contact us is via email at office@houseofhealingministries.org

⬚

Other Healing and Restoration Resources
by Jim & Pat Banks

Which Tree, by Pat Banks
Loved to Intimacy by Pat Banks
The Insidious Dance, the Paralysis of Perfectionism,
The Effects of Trauma and How to Deal With It, 3rd Edition
Helping Your Veteran Deal With the Effects of Trauma
One Calling, One Ministry
Defeating Jezebel
Finishing Well
Angels and Demons
Cast A Long Shadow
Finding Your Life Calling
Boundaries
Just Thinking
Sex Trafficking Ministry Manual, by Jim Banks & Becca Wineka
Angels & Demons
All of the above titles are available at www.amazon.com

You might also like to subscribe to Jim's blog on
www.houseofhealingministries.org or listen to various audio
versions of the Trauma Prayer at www.traumaprayer.com.

Acknowledgements:

We would like to gratefully thank a few of the people and ministries for their commitment to the body of Christ in helping to bring healing, wholeness and maturity to broken people across the world. These individuals and their ministries have been instrumental in our own lives and ministry, as well as in that of many others, for their sacrifices and insight into working with issues of the human heart and spirit. Whether it has been through reading their books and publications, listening to teachings, attending their trainings, or receiving personal ministry, they have all in some way helped us on our journey and contributed to the body of knowledge and experiences that we operate through today. Our hope is that we have been good stewards of all they have poured out.

John and Paula Sandford, www.elijahhouse.org, Couer d'Alene, ID
Derrin Carmack (deceased) formerly of Windsor, CO
Jack and Trisha Frost, www.shilohplace.org, North Myrtle Beach, SC
JoAnn Arizaga, Friend & Mentor, Elizabeth City, NC
Arthur Burk, www.theslg.com, Spartanburg, SC
Dr. Tom Hawkins, www.rcm-usa.org, Grottoes, VA
Fr Andrew Miller, HeartSync Ministries, Tallahassee, FL
Dr. Paul Cox, www.aslansplace.com, Hisperia, CA
Ed Smith, www.theophostic.com

Made in the USA
Columbia, SC
30 August 2018